All rights reserved. Without limiting the rights under copyright reserved. No part of this book may be reproduced, stored in or introduced into a retrieval system, or transmitted, in any form, or by an means (electronic, mechanical, photocopying, recording or otherwise) without prior written consent from the author Elaine Lee or the publisher Exposed Books Publishing, except for brief quotes used in reviews. For information regarding special discounts or bulk purchases, please contact Elaine Lee at info@offtocollegebookofknowledge.com or Exposed Books Publishing at info@exposedbooks.com.

Copyright © (2011) by Elaine Lee

ISBN – 978-0-9854489-2-9
Library of Congress Control Number 2019909732
Off To College Book Of Knowledge
Written by: Elaine Lee
Publishing by: Exposed Books Publishing
Text Formation by: Elaine Lee and Exposed Books Publishing
Cover Design by: Oliva ProDesigns
Printed in the United States of America

OFF TO COLLEGE………BOOK OF KNOWLEDGE

Are You Ready To Become An
Independent Woman?

A workbook of your College Journey

A Journey of Growth, Independence, Self-Control,
Self-Discovery and Womanhood.

ELAINE LEE

Off To College...Book Of Knowledge!

CONTENTS
ACKNOWLEDGMENTS
INTRODUCTION……………………………………………..

VISION & MISSION STATEMENT……………..………….

1. **A NEW START** …………………………………………pg. 7
   My First Day of College

2. **CHECK- IN** …………………………………………...pg. 11
   Where Is My Room?

3. **TAKE NOTE**……………………………………….…pg. 14
   Write It Down

4. **WHO ARE YOU** ……………………………………...pg. 24
   What Type of Person Am I?

5. **WHAT YOU NEED TO KNOW**…………………….…pg. 30
   Campus Information

6. **AFFIRMATIONS**……………………………………. pg. 49
   Positive Thinking

7. **SELF DEVELOPMENT**……………………………….pg. 54
   Working On Me

8. **SEX/HEALTH/DATING**……………………………...pg. 60
   My Life

9. **DOMESTICS**………………………………….….…pg. 70
   What Is That Smell?

10. **ETIQUETTE**……………………………………...pg. 75
    What Is Proper Etiquette?

Off To College...Book Of Knowledge!

WELCOME TO YOUR EXCITING JOURNEY!

Every young lady entering college should have this guide. Each and every one of you are here for the same reason, to get an education. Many of you entering college are going to be scared, alone and vulnerable, but in time it will pass. This is a new chapter in your life.

No more mom screaming, *"get up you are going to be late for school or you are not wearing that to school."* College is about independence and you being your own boss. ARE YOU READY? Will you get up on time, eat breakfast, get dressed and get yourself to class by yourself? Yes, I said by yourself. No more people telling you what to do. No more chores to do before you can go out with your friend and no more you're grounded. YOU ARE YOUR OWN BOSS NOW! Can you handle the responsibility?

College can be overwhelming and it will be from time to time. All the school work, classes, finding a job, friends and peer pressure belong to you. So, what are you going to do about all of this responsibility? Take a moment to think about it. You finally got your wish. All those years of saying, **"I can't wait until I'm 18, than I can do what I want."**

Congratulations, your wait is over!

After you have your attack of fear, calm down. The answers to all of your questions are in this book. Keep this book with you at all times. Remember every day is a new day and new journeys are waiting that's full of possibilities. This book is to help you in your decision making process. *SO RELAX*!

I knew there would be a lot of young ladies in need of this book and looking for answers too many questions.

This book is also about learning to take care of yourself and control of your life. Enjoy it! You can be confident in knowing that having this book can help you improve your critical thinking skills and decision making. Take your time to make decisions and look at the pros and cons of your decisions. This is your chance to think as an adult.

Enjoy your college journey. It will not be easy and there will be some bumps in the road, but trust yourself and go for it. This is an amazing opportunity to take control of your future starting now.

Again, be mindful of the choices you make and remember it's easy to get into trouble, but...... it takes so much to get out.

Keep in mind you're an adult now and whenever you get arrested for any incident that occurred on or off campus, it will be on your permanent record. This could affect you getting a job after graduation. To you it could be a minor offense, but to an employer doing your background check it shows that you are irresponsible and that is not the type of individual that a company would want to hire to represent their company.

Know that you are there for an education and remain focused on the goal of graduation.

You do not have to plan your life around this book, just plan to have it in your life.

Your goal is to either:

Learn college life or **FAIL.**

Educate yourself or **FAIL.**

Get "can't" out of your vocabulary or you will **FAIL.**

Learn to be productive in society and achieve your goals or **FAIL.**

College is not easy, but having a plan and being organized can make college life fun and exciting........................ARE YOU READY TO SUCCEED?

Off To College...Book Of Knowledge!

VISION

To guide young ladies in their growth/informative stages to Womanhood.

MISSION

To educate young ladies to become empowered and independent young women.

Ladies,

Below is the formula for success. Remember it or post it with your affirmations. When you combine all of these elements together, your only option is **Success.**

Formula For Success

Focus Driven (Consistency + Hardwork) = SUCCESS

Time

$$\frac{FD}{T}(C+HW) = S$$

CHAPTER 1
A NEW START

The key to enjoying college is a positive attitude. For many this will mean a new attitude. Yes ladies, we all have attitudes and it can be dangerous if we do not learn how to control it. A new attitude is a wonderful change. Leave the high school attitude right where you learned it, in high school. College is a place to learn and a bad attitude will make the semester seem longer because you need friends and classmates to get through it.

Now, let's get down to business. College, you made it. Congratulations, you are on your way. You have taken the first step toward your collegiate career. Now, let's start off on the right path.

College can be a good experience. This is a good time when you will feel excited, meeting new people, being on your own, making decisions for yourself and making lifelong friendships.

Or........

College can be a bad experience. You are unhappy, not meeting people, partying all night, skipping class, making bad decisions, smoking, drinking and having sex with many people. There are many dangers and consequences that follow these actions.

Ladies, you are our Lawyers, Doctors, Teachers and Entrepreneurs of tomorrow, so make us proud by making good decisions.

On the next page there are some questions to ask yourself. Take your time. Days if you have to. These are some serious questions. These questions will tap into your critical thinking skills that you will have to use in many of your classes. You are in college now, so critical thinking is crucial.

Off To College...Book Of Knowledge!

Notes:

_____
_____
_____
_____

What is my purpose here at college?

_____
_____
_____
_____

Who are the people counting on me to succeed?

_____
_____
_____
_____

Off To College...Book Of Knowledge!

Will I be the first in my family to graduate from college?

_____

_____

_____

_____

How will my decisions affect me and others?

_____

_____

_____

_____

How do I want people to see me as a person?

_____

_____

_____

_____

Off To College...Book Of Knowledge!

How do I see myself? (ex. Strong, shy, outgoing etc..)

_____

_____

_____

_____

CHAPTER 2
CHECK IN, WHERE IS MY ROOM?

Where Is My Room

Moving- In! Today is the day. Your parents have come to see where you will spend the next four years of your life. They will drop you off and your stuff, jump back in their car and do the happy dance, sing and have a discussion on their way home about what to do with the extra room.

While mom wants a guest or workout room, dad wants his very own T.V. room away from everything in the house. Whatever the reason, you no longer have your own room in their home.

So, there you are, staring at the car as it disappears into the world of endless motion. Than you think to yourself how could something so big {the car} become as small as a dot in the distance?

You stand there looking around until you realize you need to get checked into your room and the only way it will happen is if you do it yourself. There you have it! Your very first decision you made on your own. So the decision making begins. Now, you need to find your room. You look around, which way do I go? Upstairs or downstairs, left or right, stairs or elevator, which way do I go?

DON'T PANIC! Take a deep breath and say I can do this. Read the directions carefully and look for signs, most likely there will be a lot of signs posted around you. Again, you have made your second decision on your own. You find your room and you realize you are the first one there.

This is your chance to pick your side of the room. There you have it, your third decision on your own in the past hour. There will be many more to come, but for now you can rest easy knowing you have a place to sleep and you worked it out on your own. Congratulations!

Off To College...Book Of Knowledge!

OK, now that you have made it this far, what's next? Brace yourself! What lies behind this door is where your life will start to change. It is called home. You know that place where all of your things are and it is your space, well this is it. You will spend your entire life(college life that is) in this little room with a stranger, can you handle it? Not sure, it's ok but you will not know until you open the door.

Now, reach for it, reach for it, turn the knob and viola! You did it, you opened the door to a new chapter in your life. Now get in there, organize your space and meet your roommate or mates if you have any. If you are one of those people who drop things wherever they go, this may be a good time, no wait this is a great time to start new and fresh and put things where they belong.

You cannot get organized if you are living in clutter. The things you do at home start to reflect on the things you do in public. Example, you throw clothes on the floor at home, you will throw trash on the street. Your important papers are all over the place in your room, than your book bag and notes will be balled up in the bottom of your book bag and your work will be wrinkled.

Something I must tell you about college. Assignment presentation is a large portion of your grade. Professors and instructors do not want you to hand in ***wrinkled in the bottom of my bag*** work. They want you to hand in well-articulated assignments.

Now Hear This, **"THERE IS NO EXTRA CREDIT IN COLLEGE"**

"Enter as *Young Ladies* leave as *Young Women*!

This may be the first time you have to do for yourself or you may have always been independent. In either case, you will need to remind yourself daily, **One Day At A Time.**

In high school someone always told you what to do, when to do it and how to do it. Well, no more rules. You are the boss of you. There are however rules to follow that are a part of adulthood.

<u>***There will always be rules!!!!!!!!!!!!!***</u>

Now get some sleep! You should be very tired from all the unpacking, checking in and all the decisions you made today. Tomorrow is a new day and a lot of decision making will occur as well.. (ex: where are all my classes and which way do I go to get to class on time.) So, take a deep breath, relax and catch some zzzzzzzzzzzzzzzzzz

Chapter 3
GET ORGANIZED

Write It Down

I find that having a journal can be your best friend when you are new to change. My journal has helped me a lot through my college days. Make it a habit to write when you are inspired, have thoughts or just feel homesick. Your journal can be your best friend and a reference book to see how your life is forever revolving and to remember the good times, bad times or just memories.

Your journal should be with you at all times. Carry it as if it was your identification. Use it every day when you need to express yourself or when you feel like writing about your daily events. For some, having a journal is easier than talking to other people about your problems.

Your first few weeks are going to be hard on you. Learning your schedule, Professors and campus grounds can be a bit overwhelming. Relax! Just remember, change is good and this is a new chapter in your life and you will learn your way quickly.

Your journal can also give you the opportunity to see how you have changed from your first day of college until your graduation day. Writing in your journal can also help you learn creative writing and critical thinking that can help you through your college classes. Always write down how you feel. If you had a bad day or a good day it will feel good to write it down.

As soon as you get your class schedule, start writing on your calendar. It is easier to get control of your semester if all of your work is right in front of you. Each class should give you a (syllabus) list of your assignments and due dates.

Dorm organization plays a major role in your learning. So, create a space that is clutter free and clean, so you can focus on what's important. **Your Education**!

Off To College...Book Of Knowledge!

College is a whole new world and there is no comparison between college and high school. Even titles and language are different. Teachers are in high school and Professors are in college.

High School teachers tolerate and excuse missed work and behavior a lot from students. Professors will fail you, no conference needed and will move on with their next class. College is not the place for games when it comes to your education, make it your number one priority.

I know how excited you are, but do not lose focus. You know you can go to college and have a baby. Yes, I said baby. You think you're grown, guys are everywhere and you go out, get drunk and do not remember what happened the next day. **DANGEROUS, DANGEROUS**. It happens all the time and in many cases, some girls are Raped. Just remember getting pregnant or being a rape victim was not in your plan of organization.

Stick to the basics and get the job done and move to the next level of learning! Be Smart, Be Intelligent, Be Independent, BE YOU!

REMEMBER: Be true to your journal and your journal will help you be true to you!

College can be a lot easier if you write everything down. This may seem unnecessary, but trust me you need this. Start your day with a plan. If you have a day when you do not have anything planned, than write on your calendar free day. This means no studying or no classes, just me time. Trust me, you will need a lot of me time. Finals can wreak havoc on you.

Get yourself organized and on track to survive the semester. If you do not plan, you will find yourself behind and struggling.

Organized: on the straight path

Unorganized: confusion going in all directions or running in circles

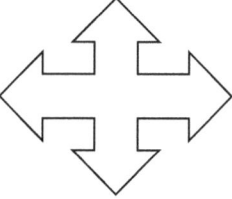

<u>*WHICH ONE ARE YOU!*</u>

This form will help you get organized and write down what you need.

Ladies, know the difference between need and want.

A need is a necessity: A basic requirement, something essential. Ex.(food, shelter, etc..)

A want is a desire: Ex.(a pair of Gucci Sunglasses)

Off To College...Book Of Knowledge!

Notes:

Things I Need

vs

Things I Want

(Never Borrow) any personal Hygiene products. (Mascara, Lip Gloss) This is a great way to pass on Infections and Germs.

NEEDS	**WANTS**
Deodorant/ Toothpaste /Food	Uggs/Lashes/Hair

Be honest with yourself. It is ok to desire things, just do not make material possessions your main priority in life.

There will be lots of questions you will ask yourself:

Who is depending on me to succeed?

Will I fail?

Will I be the first person in my family to graduate?

How will my decisions affect other people?

Can I do this?

Will I survive college?

Will I Graduate from College?

STOP: Take A Deep Breath, Count to 10, and Relax. You can do this.

Life is full of questions, welcome to the real world of adulthood.

Just remember this is normal, there is nothing wrong with you. If you do not feel overwhelmed or scared than it means you have yourself organized, you are in control and ready to face any challenge that comes your way.

Use the worksheet below to help you organize your questions and answers of the people supporting you through your journey to becoming a college

Off To College...Book Of Knowledge!

graduate. Hang this in a place where you can use it as motivation when things seem to be a bit hard on you and you feel like you cannot make it. College is not easy and every day you will grow. Remember to just give yourself time. Stick to the ultimate plan, graduation day.

List your Questions:

Example:

Who has sacrificed for me to be here?
Dad/ Grandparents/Aunt Leslie/ Brother Larry

Off To College...Book Of Knowledge!

| |
| |

| |
| |

Life is a revolving circle and you must be able to roll with what life gives you. Below is a circle of movement. Each day you will encounter something new and you need to put into practice how you will handle situations that occur. It is important that you understand college life. It's tough and there will be times when you are going to want to quit. KEEP GOING!!! You are there because you worked hard and someone decided to give you a chance. Nothing in life worth having comes easy, you have to fight hard for what you want.

Now, start your visualization chart and put in your three important questions to help you get started.

   examples:

                How will I handle situations that are out of my control?

                What steps do I need to take to make things happen for me?

                How can I become more involved in my progress at college?

Off To College...Book Of Knowledge!

Think of some questions of your own to achieve.

Rank from most important to least important.

1.
2.
3.
4.
5.
6
7.
8.
9
10.

Off To College...Book Of Knowledge!

Notes:

_____

_____

_____

_____

_____

_____

_____

_____

_____

_____

_____

_____

_____

_____

_____

CHAPTER 4
WHO ARE YOU?

Who Are You?

What Type Of Person Am I?

Take a moment to think about these questions.

Who are you?

Answering these questions will help you work on who you are and who you want to be.

Dig deep down inside yourself and think of the way you have been living your life. Are you happy with what you see?

Think back to when you did something good and how it made you feel. Now, think of a time when you did something bad and how it made you feel? These types of questions will help you with your critical thinking skills that you will need throughout your collegiate career and beyond. So, starting early is a good step in the right direction.

Below is a Type chart rated A thru E. Write down all that applies to you. If you are any of the negatives, than you have some work to do to make them positives.

Type Chart

- **Type A (positive)** Awesome - You remember special occasions of all your friends, you send birthday cards and wishes. You love to get together with your friends and you see the good in every situation.

- **Type B (negative)** Bitchy- Everything thing is your way or else. You are the center of attention or else. You never have anything positive to say about anyone else. You are mean to your friends.

- **Type C (positive)** Concerned- You care about people and you put others before your needs. You hurt when your friends hurt. You always want to help when you can. You are a giver.

- **Type D (negative)** Deceitful - You are a liar. You lie to keep friends and you lie on your friends. You lie about everything to get people to like you. (If this is you, stop.) You are hurting people because you are hurting. No one wants to be around you, not the person you pretend to be.

❏ **Type E (positive)** Empowering - You empower people. You are a great support system. You are a cheerleader for the team. Everyone comes to you for help. You are positive energy.

Notes:

Do not change who you are to be someone's friend. We are all individuals and do not try to change someone else to fit your needs, it never works.

Ladies a few rules to follow:

1. Mind your own business. If you are not directly involved in what is happening, stay out of it.
2. **YOU ARE IN COLLEGE NOW, LEAVE HIGH SCHOOL BEHIND.**
3. Gossip destroy friendships. If you have a friend who always talks about others, tell her how you feel about it and if she continues to do it, walk away.
4. Remember you are judged by the company you keep. Choose your friends wisely.
5. Be your own boss. You are an individual. Do not be quick to want to join the most popular group of girls. There can only be one leader. You were not accepted into college to be part of the most popular girl group. You were accepted into college because of your hard work, not popularity in high school. Continue to do the hard work, think for yourself and you will be fine

5 Steps to remember to succeed. These can also be used as Affirmations.

1. **Know what you want**
2. **Believe in what you want**
3. **Do not accept Defeat or NO**
4. **Be persistent**
5. **Go for it**

REMEMBER: IT's ALWAYS GOOD TO BE A LEADER THAN A FOLLOWER

Off To College...Book Of Knowledge!

Set time aside for yourself every day. Life moves at such a fast pace and we need time to slow down, catch our breath and breathe easy.

Get organized and buy a planner to keep you on track. A planner will help you keep your appointments and know your schedule daily. Being organized will also keep you on schedule with all of your class assignments that you will do.

Most schools may provide a planner for you. If not they are very reasonably priced and come in many different colors and sizes. **NO EXCUSES!!!!!!**

NOTES:

_____

_____

_____

_____

_____

_____

_____

_____

_____

Off To College...Book Of Knowledge!

Chapter 5
What You Need To Know

Be sure to check your school's vision and mission statement. This will let you know what your school prides itself on and what it expects to accomplish.

Your job is to make sure your school lives up to their statements. If you feel your school does not meet the expectations as written, talk to your school president.

Check your school student activities board or front desk to keep yourself informed on what is going on at the campus. Too often, many students never know what is happening and they miss out on important information and events.

Listed below is a breakdown of the topics covered in this section. Chapter 5 is very important. Pay close attention to each section. I suggest you think about starting a GLO Chapter on campus. These topics should be your focus of discussion daily; regardless of your race, background or sexual orientation. At the end of the day, we are all girls and safety is the number one priority. From your first day until your last day, these topics will and should always be at the forefront of discussion. Make sure you use these topics until you graduate from college. This chapter will allow you to keep notes and keep track of your progress. Good Luck!

Topics:

1. **Girl Link Organization, Inc. (G.L.O.) - www.girllink.org**
2. **Student Enforced Safety Patrol:** S.E.S.P
3. **Your Level: Freshman/Sophomore/Junior/Senior**
4. **S.E.L.F.:** Stop* Exhale* Let It Go*Forget About It

Off To College...Book Of Knowledge!

Girl Link Organization, Inc. (G.L.O.)

G.L.O. Is a program designed to tackle all issues young ladies face daily.

Below is a list of topics covered in the program:

- Self-Improvement/Self Esteem
- Sex/Health/Dating/Safety
- Beauty/Proper Dressing
- Finances
- Etiquette/Domestic Skills/ Life Skills
- Respect/ Friendship/Bullying
- Applying For Jobs/Resume Writing/Interviewing

If your school does not offer this program; get your girls together, start a Chapter and put in a request to your student activities department head. This is a great idea to have for RA's.

Student Enforced Safety Patrol

<u>S.E.S.P.</u>

Pay Close Attention: **YOUR SAFETY IS IMPORTANT**

I repeat : **YOUR SAFETY IS IMPORTANT**

Ladies get on patrol. Your safety is important. Too many sexual assaults are happening on campuses and not being reported. It is imperative to get on board and take your safety seriously! So, get some girls together and start a Safety Patrol Chapter at your school. More information is available at www.girllink.org.

Off To College...Book Of Knowledge!

NOTES:

Off To College...Book Of Knowledge!

FRESHMAN

Congratulations, and welcome to year one. Let's do all the things to get you through the 1st semester, which is the hardest and get you through the year. Below are 10 very important things you should know.

Thank your parents for getting you through high school and to your 1st year!

1. You are going to experience fear for a while and it's ok. It is part of the package deal and learning. You are in a new environment and fear is a natural response. Give it time, it will pass.

2. Have a plan of organization ready. If you do not have one, get it done now! As soon as you settle down in your room. (Get a planner, write down your classes and study your schedule immediately.)

3. As soon as you get your syllabus(class schedule) get your planner out and write down your assignment due dates.

4. Establish a friendship with your roommate. You are going to be spend every night in your space with this person, get to know them. Be respectful of your dorm space. Remember you are sharing with someone else.
*(If you feel you are having an issue with your living quarters, handle it like an adult and talk to your roommate first. If it cannot be resolved, than go to Student Housing.)

5. If you get a meal card, it is for you to eat not your friends, be responsible. In your 1st year of college, most students gain a lot of weight due to eating a lot of junk food. College cafeteria's have a lot of options and too often processed food wins.

6. Avoid dating for now. You will have enough on your plate. Your focus should be on

Off To College...Book Of Knowledge!

studying. Your first year is going to be hard on you and it is not going to be easy. Be responsible and make the right decisions for you. When making decisions give yourself time, do not rush, weigh your options, the pros and cons. You are an adult now and the decisions you make are for you and not for someone else. Always remember you have control over you, do not give that to anyone. ex. (girlfriends/boyfriends/friends)

7. Be sure to familiarize yourself with your campus. Do not rely on information from others about your surroundings. Learn all the emergency exits in your building in the event of an emergency. Know where campus police offices are.
P.S. do not find out about campus police locations due to you getting in trouble and being held there.

8. Talk to your professors if you need help. They are there to help you and give you guidance. Just remember there is no extra credit in college. Assignments are due when they are due. Keep track of your planner. Write everything down.

9. Be a leader for yourself. No hard partying. Get your schedule and studying together first before you get out and lose control. Now, I am not saying do not have fun. Know your limits and be responsible. Going to an occasional party is fine but 4 to 5 parties a week is Trouble.

10. Always, Always, Always travel with someone on campus. Do not walk alone at night. If you find yourself in this situation, call campus police for an escort to your dorm or check to see if your school has S.E.S.P. (Student Enforced Safety Patrol) If not start it yourself with your roommate. It is a great way to become well known on campus and take a stance for a great cause, the safety of all young women on campus.

- Your Freshman year and High School are not the Same. You have graduated to the next level of learning.
- Know the RED ZONE
    - The red zone is your 1st week in college and you are willing to do anything to make new friends and fit in. **Be Careful!** Do not change you in order to be someone's friend. Remember everyone will not be your friend.

Off To College...Book Of Knowledge!

Notes:

Off To College...Book Of Knowledge!

SOPHOMORE

WELCOME BACK! YOU SURVIVED THE 1ST YEAR. HOW DO YOU FEEL? NOW, LET'S GET SETTLED INTO YOUR SOPHOMORE YEAR.

OK ladies, by now you should know the layout of campus grounds and be more settled into your comfort zone away from home.

Here are a few important things you should know.

1. You made it to the next level, (a sophomore) you are now closer to the finish line. The fear you had as a freshman should be gone, but if not it's ok. However, you should feel comfortable in your space.

2. You should have your plan of organization down and together. Your planner should be full of all your class information. The same rules apply from your freshman year. You should have an idea of how your day will be scheduled. Your classes should be getting harder now. You should be taking classes in your major. If not stay on track you are doing a good job.

Please keep in mind academic probation is not good. You can be put out of school if you are not performing to school standards.

3. Again, as soon as you receive your syllabus, get that planner out and start organizing. Get everything from that syllabus written on your calendar, so you do not miss any Assignments.

*Your planner is your personal assistant, use it to keep yourself organized.

4. Establish a friendship with your roommate. Again, if you feel there may be a conflict with the living arrangements, contact student housing.

5. Get involved in campus life, join clubs that interest you. This is a great way to meet people and build friendships and relationships.

Off To College...Book Of Knowledge!

6. **Be cautious about dating.** I know there are a lot of options on campus and you want to jump right in, but wait. Remember your purpose and how much time you are going to have to put into a relationship, time you do not have. College is not the place to date. Too much temptation. Also, there are other dangers. STD's, Pregnancy, Rape, Campus Crime and Domestic Violence.

If you are going to date, be in control of you. Do not let anyone run your life or have control over you. Too often, college dating can turn into Domestic Violence and it is not reported. If you do not know; if your boyfriend or girlfriend constantly calls you names or disrespects you that is called verbal abuse.

If your mate is violent and has hit you, **TELL SOMEONE. You are not a punching bag!** Go to campus police, tell a friend, dial 911 or call me (410-881-7221) if you have too, just tell someone.

7. Remember your professors are your friends, Failure is not an option. Go to them for help.

8. Partying, failure to turn in assignments and missing classes can get you put on Academic Probation or put out of school. This stays on your college transcript, when you apply at other schools they will see it. Be responsible!

9. Please take advantage of the library. You should be spending a lot of time there. Keep your focus on studying. Party after your assignments are done.

10. *Always, Always, Always travel with someone on campus. Do not walk alone at night. If you find yourself in this situation, call campus police for an escort to your dorm or check to see if your school has SESP. (Student Enforced Safety Patrol) If not start it yourself with your roommate. It is a great way to take a stance for a great cause, the safety of all young women on campus.

Off To College...Book Of Knowledge!

Notes:

Off To College...Book Of Knowledge!

Off To College...Book Of Knowledge!

JUNIOR

YOU MADE IT. YOU ARE NOW 1 YEAR AWAY FROM GRADUATING FROM COLLEGE.

This is the time to start looking for Internships. Go to your work study department or start looking on your own.

1. You are now at the level of major decision making. You should be settled into your major and thinking about continuing on to grad school. This is a big decision.

2. Your plan of organization should be a work of art, if not then stop what you are doing and get it together now. If you need help go to www.girllink.org to get organization tips. You have had 2 years to get it together. It is time to get serious and use your planner to help you get better.

3. Again, as soon as you receive your syllabus get all of your class information on it. Studying and research should be your life now. Do not let unimportant things get you off track. Be a leader not a follower.

4. Set small goals for yourself. Finish this semester, to get to the next small goal which is the next semester. After you get all of the small goals accomplished, you reach the ultimate goal, College Graduation.

5. If you have a friend who parties all the time and constantly wants you to hang out with them during your study time, you do not need me to tell what to do. However, I will get away from them. Clearly this person is failing and they need someone to fail with them. Remember misery loves company. This is not a friend. This is a selfish person.

FAILURE IS NOT AN OPTION.

Off To College...Book Of Knowledge!

6. Before you leave for the summer check with your counselor to make sure all of your classes are in order. If not get it taken care of. Do not take the summer off if you need to make up classes.

7. Always, Always, Always travel with someone on campus. Do not walk alone at night. If you find yourself in this situation, call campus police for an escort to your dorm or check to see if your school has S.E.S.P. (Student Enforced Safety Patrol) If not start it yourself with your roommate. It is a great way to become well known on campus and take a stance for a great cause, the safety of all young women on campus. Go to www.girllink.org for your starter Information list.

Off To College...Book Of Knowledge!

Notes:

Off To College...Book Of Knowledge!

Off To College...Book Of Knowledge!

SENIOR

CONGRATULATIONS! YOU DID IT. SENIOR YEAR! LET'S GET THROUGH IT. YOU GOT THIS.

1. The 1st thing to do is to get an appointment scheduled with your counselor to make sure all of your classes are in order. You want to graduate on time. I have seen it too often the disappointment on parents faces when graduation is missed. Be responsible!

2. This is it. Pat yourself on the back you made it this far. Another small goal accomplished. It's time to put your last plan of action in motion.

3. Also, it is ok if you have to do 5 years. Some schools offer a five year program to get your Masters. If your school offers it, take it. One more year will not hurt you. You will be at Graduate Student school level.

4. Will your internship open doors to a job offer when you graduate? If so congratulations. If not get out there and start looking. Do not wait until the last minute to look for a job. Keep in mind, companies do interviews and will wait until you graduate to hire you.

5. Do you have the necessary tools for interviews. Go to www.girllink.org for the interview tool kit.

6. Attend college fairs as often as you can, but do not let it interfere with class. Keep in mind you may not find a job in your major right away, so keep an open mind if a job offer comes along.

7. Continue to stay focused on your class work. There is still a lot of work to be done.

8. Try to help a fellow classmate in their journey.(freshman, sophomore, junior or senior) Be honest with them about your struggles and dealing with campus life. Your journey could help them on theirs.

9. Go to your student Activities Advisor and let them know some things that have helped you. This may help the new students arriving.

10. Your final task as a senior, be thankful for making it! Not many of your peers you started out with have made it. Some have dropped out, flunked out, been put out or transferred out. Whatever the case may be, you made it. Go back and thank all the people who were in your corner pushing you to succeed. Let them know you appreciate them for helping you on your 4 /5 year journey.

Now, Let's get this semester over and get that cap and gown.

FINALLY FROM ME TO YOU, I AM PROUD OF YOU, WHEN THE DAY COMES AND YOU WALK ACROSS THAT STAGE AND YOUR NAME IS CALLED, KNOW THAT I AM PROUD OF YOU. YOU WORKED HARD AND YOU DESERVE THIS MOMENT BECAUSE IT IS YOURS AND NO ONE CAN TAKE THAT FROM YOU.

ENJOY YOUR MOMENT.........COLLEGE GRADUATE

Off To College...Book Of Knowledge!

Notes:

Chapter 6
AFFIRMATIONS

AFFIRMATIONS

What is an Affirmation?

An affirmation is a statement asserting the existence or truth of something. (ex.: I will graduate from college.)   (Webster Dictionary)

Positive thinking can help you through any situation.

All you have to do is believe and make a commitment to yourself and make it happen.

A good source of positive thinking is affirmations. Feel free to come up with your own and recite them every day. The best way for me to remember my affirmations, is to post them on my bathroom mirror so I can see them every morning. The ones that are the most important to me, I recite three or four times a day.

A good tip to remember:

Record them to carry with you daily. Most cell phones have a record feature.

AFFIRMATIONS FOR COLLEGE CLASSES

- I have the power to pass these classes
- I have the power to write this paper
- I am stress free
- I am happy
- I am at peace
- I will pass this test

Off To College...Book Of Knowledge!

- I will get an A in this class
- I will be responsible
- My accomplishments I control
- I will survive this semester

Create your own and write them on post it notes or write them down in your journal and say them daily.

I will _____

I will _____

I will _____

I will _____

I will _____

I will _____

I will _____

I will _____

I will _____

I will _____

I will _____

Off To College...Book Of Knowledge!

Notes:

Off To College...Book Of Knowledge!

Off To College...Book Of Knowledge!

Off To College...Book Of Knowledge!

CHAPTER 7
SELF-DEVELOPMENT

How do you feel about yourself?

TAKE A MOMENT TO THINK ABOUT YOUR ANSWER.

A.   Are you happy?

_____

_____

_____

_____

B.   Why do you feel the way you do?

_____

_____

_____

_____

C.   Do you feel unattractive?

_____

Off To College...Book Of Knowledge!

D. Are you ashamed of who you are?

PEER PRESSURE

What is peer pressure to you?

Off To College...Book Of Knowledge!

_____

_____

Do you feel you have to do things you do not want to do to fit in with the crowd?

_____

_____

_____

Remember ladies: it's better to be a leader than a follower.
> **Being a leader will get you further in life than being a follower.**

Discussion: what do I mean by this statement?

Note:

What if you and your girl were walking down the street and a group of guys pull up in a Range Rover and asked you if you would like to go to a party at their boys house? Your girl recognizes one of the guys from around the way, but she doesn't know him.

You said no thanks, but your girl said ok let's go. We're not doing anything else, let's go have some fun.

What do you do:

* A. Go have some fun
* B. Stick to your no thanks

Off To College...Book Of Knowledge!

> * C.   You pull your girl to the side and ask her what is her problem. Their idea of fun may not be the same idea of fun you are thinking about.

This is just one example of bad decision making and putting your life in danger.

GOALS

Do you have any goals set for yourself?

Ex:
Finish college
Become a teacher, doctor, nurse, lawyer
Volunteer more of my time to a charity or an organization
Open my own business

*Why do you think it's important to have goals?

Do you think you would be able to succeed without goals?

Discussion:

What are some of your goals?

_____

_____

_____

Why did you pick these goals?

_____

_____

Off To College...Book Of Knowledge!

_____

Do you think you will reach your goals?

_____

_____

_____

Are you ready for this responsibility?

_____

_____

_____

FAMILY LIFE

How do you feel about your family?

_____

_____

_____

_____

Off To College...Book Of Knowledge!

Do you have a relationship with your parents and siblings?

_____
_____
_____
_____
_____

Are you an only child? How do you feel about it?

_____
_____
_____

If you could change your family life, what would you change and why?

_____
_____
_____
_____

Off To College...Book Of Knowledge!

CHAPTER 8
SEX/HEALTH/DATING/SAFETY

It's My Life and BODY

SEX

1. Are you sexually Active? _____yes ____no
2. Have you ever had an STD (Sexually Transmitted Disease)? ___yes ___no
3. What is an STD?

Any of various diseases or infections (as syphilis, gonorrhea, chlamydia, and genital herpes) that are usually transmitted by direct sexual contact and that include some (as hepatitis B and AIDS) that may be contracted by other than sexual means.

Merriam-Webster Online Dictionary

4. If you had/have an STD, it is important to get professional help from a doctor. Please check your school information to find the campus doctor's office.

It is an embarrassing situation, but if you do not get checked it can lead to major health issues.

(herpes: incurable; AIDS- Life threatening; Infertility)

5. What is your definition of sex?

_____

_____

_____

_____

6. Your body is your temple! Treat it well. Be concerned with what goes into your body.

> College will allow you to see your classmates male and female do some pretty stupid, daring and wild things. Do not let sex be your problem. Keep in mind, yes there are boys and girls everywhere and maybe they all have slept with several people there.

7. If you think you have an STD, see a doctor as soon as possible. You need to start the healing process before you do some serious damage to your body.

> Are you a virgin?   ____ yes   ____ no

Being a virgin is not a bad thing. In fact, it is the best thing. Have sex when you are ready. This is a decision you need to think long and hard on. Do not be rushed into sex, if you are not ready.

Sex for the first time should be special. Be sure the person you are with deserves you.

> There will be a lot of broken hearts in college. Girls as well as guys are going to get excited and *lose their minds* from all the dating opportunities. It's a trap, don't fall for it.

You are in college to get an education in learning, not sex acts. Control yourself, the semester will be long and hard and your concentration should be on **the books not sex.**

Below is a list of STD's to research

There are many types of Sexually Transmitted Diseases and unfortunately not all of them have symptoms that are easily detected, especially for women. It is so important to **practice safe sex** (http://www.menstruation.com.au/periodpages/avoidstd.html) and to have regular doctor visits if you are sexually active with multiple partners or serial (done several times) partners.

It's time to be honest with yourself. Your health and the way you treat your body is your responsibility. Be aware of what you put in it and what comes out!

Some signs and symptoms of STD's include

- sores or blisters around the sex organs or mouth
- swelling, pain or itchiness around sex organs
- pain or burning during urination *you could also have a UTI(urinary tract infection)
- discharge from the vagina that smells

Remember you can have an STD without having any symptoms at all and you can't tell if someone else has an STD just by looking at them. Unless, they have breakouts. Know the signs.

Commonly known STD's are:

- AIDS (Acquired Immune Deficiency Syndrome)
- Genital Warts
- Gonorrhea
- Syphilis
- Herpes
- **Chlamydia** *most common
- Pubic Lice or Crabs
- Vaginitis
- Hepatitis

Getting Tested

If you have any of the symptoms listed above - see your doctor or family planning clinic and get tested immediately. Most STD's can be treated if they are diagnosed quickly enough. However if the STD's are left untreated severe complications do occur.

For females - apart from getting tested if you spot any STD signs or symptoms **it is a good idea to get tested between partners** to ensure that early detection is possible.

Also check out **www.teensource.com** it is a great resource link.

Off To College...Book Of Knowledge!

NOTES:

Health

Do you think you are healthy? ____yes   ____no

Do you know what healthy is? ___yes   ____no

College can wreak havoc on your eating habits. Let's be real you have horrible eating habits.

You eat fast food, fried food, desserts, candy snacks: translation sophomore food, greasy food, sugar, sugar and more sugar. Having poor eating habits can cause a downward spiral to your health, self-esteem and grades.

When your eating habits are bad you will gain weight. College can cause you to eat out a lot. Ordering take out, eating on the go or just not caring about what you eat will put the pounds on you. Be careful and mindful of what you're eating. Eating affects your emotional state. The more you eat and not exercise, the more weight you will gain.

Let's try an activity.

1. Weigh yourself first thing in the morning after you use the bathroom and before you eat or drink anything.

2. Do not weigh yourself again until the 14th day after you repeat step 1.

3. Continue with your regular routine and eat the way you normally do. Except no bread, sugar or processed food.

4. No Cheating!!!!! Do not weigh yourself until the 14th day.

What is your weight now: Day 1: ____   Day 14: ___

<u>***Once you cut all of the junk food out, sugar and soda you will be surprised at the number***</u>.

GOOD LUCK!

Weight gain can also cause you to be ashamed of your body. When you gain weight your self-esteem goes down. People start saying, girl you gained some weight.

Holiday time and going home is the worst. When you go home to see family and friends for the first time since you left, the weight gain can be a shock to them. You will hear from time to time, *girl you got fat or you gained some weight*. Don't panic, it happens all the time. This is why I wrote this book.

When you get back to school, start a new plan to eat nutritional meals. The school cafeteria has healthy food to eat. Stay away from eating junk food. Limit your cheat day to once a week, when you can have whatever you want.

Remember everything should be done in moderation. Eat when you are hungry not when your friends say let's go out to eat. JUST SAY NO !!! It is not a bad word.

Eat lots of fruits and vegetables and carry fruit and healthy snacks in your bag to keep you from stopping at fast food restaurants.

This is a new change in your life just as going off to college. Embrace it. Love yourself and keep a healthy body inside and out.

If you have girlfriends, start something new on campus. Get them together and start a campaign for healthy eating and living. Help your classmates make healthy choices as well. It could help you and your girls make an impact on campus life.

Off To College...Book Of Knowledge!

NOTES:

DATING:

You are not a punching bag

Dating can be exciting and also dangerous. Let's keep it real! College gives you the opportunity to see many options when dating. Lots of guys and girls to choose from. BE CAREFUL!!!

Remember what you are in college for. People are counting on you to make it so do what you are there to do. I would suggest not dating your first semester or year. You will have enough time to date once you have been there for some time.

Trust me the dating pool will always be there.

Before you jump into a serious relationship, check out these websites to know the warning signs of an abusive relationship. These websites are an excellent source and you should pass it on to your friends.

www.breakthecycle.org

www.loveisrespect.org

www.teensource.org

These websites will open your eyes to protecting yourself as well as teach you the warning signs of an abusive relationship. Are you the abuser?

BE CAREFUL!! Protect yourself at all times.

If you are in an abusive relationship tell someone as soon as possible. Report it to the school police, your counselor or the crisis hotline at you school. Just tell someone who can help you get out.

Know that it is not your fault. No one deserves to be abused, you are not someone's property. Abuse can come in many forms.

Off To College...Book Of Knowledge!

Below are just two to be aware of

Physical: grabbing, touching, shoving, hitting, punching, etc.....

Verbal: name calling, yelling constantly in your face, attacking your character, etc.....

If you are in a relationship and can relate to any of these issues, it is time to get out now. Do not try to give reasons as to why you are being abused. You cannot change people. You can only control you.

Make your safety and well-being your #1 priority.

For immediate assistance or to talk to a trained advocate:

Call the National Teen Dating Abuse Helpline
Love Is Respect
**24 hours a day at
1-866-331-9474
[1-866-331-8453 TTY]**

Notes:

_____

_____

_____

_____

_____

_____

Off To College...Book Of Knowledge!

Chapter 9
Domestic: What is that smell?

You open the door to your room and pewwwwwww! Where is that smell coming from? It is a nasty embarrassing smell. You cannot seem to find it. Keep looking you are getting closer, closer, closer you've found it. ***It's your room!***

When was the last time you cleaned your room? I mean really cleaned it. Your room is a reflection of you. If your room has dirty clothes and trash everywhere, chances are your room stinks. Let's be real.

You are in college now so act like it. Get organized. If you live in clutter, then your life will be an unorganized mess. It's time you start acting like a young adult and take control of your life.

You should be ready to settle yourself down and imagine yourself out of college, living alone and having your own stuff. College is a great place for you to get the training and experience of being independent. Even if you have a roommate(s) the way you keep your area clean will help you in the long run, trust me.

Sit down and get yourself on a schedule. Write down the days you will wash clothes and clean your space. Remember girls, college is a place of learning, growing and maturing.

Get on track and get yourself organized, so college can be a great experience not a horrible stage in your life.

Having domestic skills is a plus for you. It does not look good or sound good when women say, "I do not know how to clean or excuse the mess." Really! Young Ladies, this is unacceptable.

Off To College...Book Of Knowledge!

I do not think you want to hear people say this about you.

Girl_____(Your Name) is a nice person, but her room is nasty, so she is probably nasty.

Get it together!

Get the skills you need to keep your dorm clean and clutter free.

Make sure you keep a cleaning schedule handy to update and post weekly. It is important to start these habits now, than to be an adult and not know.

If you did not have the responsibility of cleaning up after yourself in high school, shame on you. You should have some form of experience cleaning up after yourself when you made a mess. Well, if you have none you're in luck. Through YES you will learn.

Remember to visit www.girllink.org for more information on etiquette tips.

THE WHITE GLOVE TEST

There are two parts to the White Glove Experience.

<u>Part 1</u>

WHITE

Try the white glove experience.

The way you keep your dorm is a reflection of you.
W- wash clothes and linens daily
H- healthy eating and living
I- iron clothing and hang up
T- put trash where it belongs
E- use eco-friendly cleaning products
Remember this daily to keep your dorm clean and germs down. It isn't healthy to allow fungus to grow on things.   Be Clean……..Young Ladies

Wash

Wash your clothes and linens. Linen should be washed every week and clothing should be washed every two weeks.

Healthy Eating

Eating healthy can help you get through college and maintain a healthy weight. Start as soon as possible and take advantage of the gym and take vitamins.

Iron

Wearing wrinkled clothing is not acceptable.

This is the time to get organized, wear clean pressed clothes, wash and fold and put them away. Organization.

Trash

Trash belongs in the trash bin. The floor is not the trash can. Allowing your dorm to look like a trash dump is not ladylike.

Eco-friendly

While in college do something good for the environment. Use eco-friendly cleaning products. Using chemicals can be harmful to your health and your living environment.

PART 2

THE WHITE GLOVE WIPE

Here's a simple test to take to see how clean your room is.

Put on a white glove and wipe your hand across any surface to see how clean it is.

Off To College...Book Of Knowledge!

If your glove is clean after you wipe your hands across the surface, Great Job! Your space is clean.

However, if you wipe your hands across any surface and it is dirty, you know what you need to do, get to cleaning. Remember to use eco-friendly cleaning products.

CHAPTER 10
ETIQUETTE

What is Etiquette?

Etiquette is not a set of rules, it's everyday living, you cannot be productive in society without it!
-Elaine Lee

Etiquette is something you need to use every day. It's not just about knowing what knife and fork to use.
It's about knowing the proper way of doing things. There are many different forms of etiquette. Business, social, phone, conversational, customer service, communication, etc.

As you mature, you will understand the importance of etiquette. When you become an adult there are things that you will learn that are expected of you. Etiquette is not a set of rules, it is everyday living, you cannot be productive in society without it. As a young lady, you should know by now the behaviors that are ladylike and acceptable and that are not ladylike and are unacceptable. Below is a breakdown chart of acceptable and unacceptable behavior.

Acceptable	Unacceptable
_____Yes_____	_____Yeah or Yup_____
_____No_____	_____Naw or Nope_____
_____	_____
_____	_____

Notes:
_____

Off To College...Book Of Knowledge!

Interviewing Tool Kit: Need to Know Interviewing Tips

Go to: www.girllink.org for interviewing tips. Click on interviewing link.

Ladies I've seen this happen time and time again when you show up for interviews and you are unprepared.

An interview is your chance to show an employer what you are made of. First impressions are lasting. Your appearance can make or break their decision.

Below is a list of 10 do's and don'ts for interviewing.

<u>10 Do's</u>

1. Get yourself prepared the night before. Your entire outfit and everything you will be taking with you.
2. Have 3 extra copies of your resume with you. Make sure all spelling is correct.
3. Arrive 15 minute early.
4. Always wear a suit. (black, grey, dark blue)
5. Wear black stockings or skin tone.
6. Cover all visible piercings and tattoos.
7. Wear shoes with a heel of 2-3 inches no higher. Black!
8. Wear nude makeup and soft lips. (no gum chewing)
9. Wear average length nails.
10. No cell phone out while waiting and Be you.

<u>10 Don'ts</u>

1. Do not wait until the morning of the interview to decide what to wear.
2. Do not go to the interview assuming the employer printed your resume.
3. Do not arrive before 15 minutes, any time before or after is unacceptable.
4. Never wear tank tops, cut out shoulders or skirts with high slits.
5. No color tights or fish nets.

Off To College...Book Of Knowledge!

6. No nose or tongue rings.
7. No open toe or 5 inch heels. No colors!
8. No color lipstick. ex. Blue/ Green
9. No long nails. They can show an employer you cannot do your job.
10. Do not go into your interview acting like someone else, saying you can do all these things you cannot do.

Notes:

Off To College...Book Of Knowledge!

Notes:

Off To College...Book Of Knowledge!

Notes:

Off To College...Book Of Knowledge!

Notes:

Off To College...Book Of Knowledge!

Notes:

Off To College...Book Of Knowledge!

Off To College...Book Of Knowledge!

Victory

A Graduation Message

It's Graduation Time! I hope your journey was full of wonder, excitement, joy, relationships made and friendships to last a lifetime. I am proud of you for hanging in there when times were rough. You never gave up and you fought for this moment. Only you could have done this for yourself. Stand tall, hold your head up high and know if no one told you this today or ever, I Am Proud of You! Job well done.

I leave you with this. The world is not an easy place, but you have the power to create your journey. Never accept defeat and keep pushing for your dreams. No one knows you like you and no knows your dreams better than you. Align yourself with people who can help you and not hinder you. As always if you need to talk or have a question please chat on the www.girllink.org site and get connected!

Ms. Elaine

Off To College...Book Of Knowledge!

What have you learned about yourself throughout your 4 or 5 year journey? Reflect back to your first day, then your last day. Go back and read your notes and discover how your writing and thinking has changed. Now, write a letter to the freshman you from the Graduate you. What will you tell her? How has she grown and matured? You will surprise yourself when you are done.

Notes:

Off To College...Book Of Knowledge!

Off To College...Book Of Knowledge!

Off To College...Book Of Knowledge!

New journeys await! Get out there and make your mark on the world.

ABOUT THE AUTHOR

Elaine Lee is an advocate for girls. With her love of helping and mentoring she has found her niche in the system. Nurturing and guiding girls to see their full potential has always been her passion. As the Founder of her Non Profit Girl Link Organization, LLC, (GLO), Elaine is able to reach more young ladies other than just in a classroom setting, on the importance of proper etiquette and the do's and don'ts of being a girl. The etiquette training program does more than teach the proper way of holding a fork. It was designed to feed the souls of young girls and give them the tools necessary to be productive in society.

With an uncanny ability to reach girls from ages 8-24, it is a blessing to be able to communicate with them. Although the age difference varies, the message is the same. Always conduct yourself as a young lady because at the end of the day the question to ask yourself is, "did I represent us (girls) well today."

Please visit www.offtocollegebookofknowledge.com to order your books and get more tips on the importance of being a girl.

Off To College...Book Of Knowledge!

www.ingramcontent.com/pod-product-compliance
Lightning Source LLC
Chambersburg PA
CBHW080924170426
43201CB00016B/2262